GW01311537

Axelle's website:

www.themetamorphicway.com

Acknowlegments

My newsletters have put a smile on people's face for years now so I hope this will do just the same for you.

Someone once told me:" You write like you speak". I hope I do, as I seem to make people feel better, uplifted and ready to "kick ass" again so let's get started.

But before we do, I want to thank all of you for sharing your troubles, showing your vulnerability and opening your heart to me. You've all inspired me and helped me find my Truth. Those lessons were priceless and still are so THANK YOU.

Also, a big thank you to the talented Gita Patel (http://www.peelmysatsuma.com) for creating my beautiful logo.

Last but not least, a huge thank you to my soul family and blood related one, you are my rock and I love you so deeply.

For your own comfort, this book consists of two parts: Body and Mind&Spirit.

Dedicated to all of you who have the courage to grow and expand.

You are my inspiration.

BODY

Breathe

First thing first, breathe. Sounds silly, doesn't it as without breathing, there wouldn't be much life left therefore no point reading about keeping your sanity or not. However, when stressed, our breath becomes short and fast so unless you are running for your life chased by a dinosaur as well as reading this...then slow down your breathing. Well done for your capacity to multitask by the way. Impressive indeed! Many people don't know how to breathe properly, another thing that should be taught at school. So, inhale deeply filling up your stomach then your chest, hold it then reverse exhaling from your chest first then emptying your stomach completely. Not our sexiest hours, I must say however you'll feel calm and collected ready to tackle any dinosaurs or other beasts. I won't name anyone.

Body talks

Reconnect with your body: it is the reality of you in this world. Sit in silence each day and LISTEN inwards. Your body talks. Use your journey on the tube and feel your body inwards. Breathe through any aches & pains. Your body is always in the present. Listen to what it has to say to you.

Smile

Take a 10-30 min walk a day. It will keep your mind clear and your body healthy. And as you walk along, just smile. Others won't mind as they are too busy with their own life. Or you might inspire them to do the same... Who can resist that smile of yours? Smile to Life and Life will smile right back at you! Positivity is infectious.

Alkaline body

Under stress, the body becomes acidic which is the root of numerous diseases. So, add some freshly squeezed lemon to warm water and drink this first thing in the morning. You will detox your liver and keep the PH of your body alkaline. I personally drink water with lemon all day long. You can support your liver by sprinkling your food with Rosemary and drink Dandelion Tea. Eat potatoes, avocados, banana, almonds, lettuce, cucumbers, carrots, celery, goat cheese, olive oil, oily fish like salmon and so much more.

TLC

Treat your body with respect, you only have one. Be kind to it. Scrub it, polish it...love it. Focus on all the parts you love...yes you do! Love it and it will love you back. Don't judge it so harshly. How often do you see the best of your body? How often do you criticize it instead? Be the best friend of your body. Tell your body that it smells nice and its skin is glowing however if it's time to come down on chocolate...Just say so. May be recommend Fennel tea after each meal to reduce water retention and any extra pounds. Be kind to your body. It's always been there for you no matter what. A real trooper!

Tree

After a busy day: stand up, feet together, arms along your body, close your eyes and stay still until your body stops swinging like a tulip in the wind. It might take a while or not however your mind will find peace. You will feel centred, grounded and calm. Enjoy your evening!

Dehydration

Heat, stress, exercise, heating system, normal sweat, all lead to dehydration and water sometimes is not enough to keep us going. Why not eating watermelon, cucumbers, celery, strawberries and drinking fruit and veggie smoothes or the legendary coconut water? Don't forget herbal teas which can be exciting like liquorice, fennel, nettle, peppermint and thyme. Who gets excited about herbal teas...? Me apparently. Don't worry, I'm going to lie down for a while, I'll be fine. In the meantime, keep hydrated and say goodbye to headaches, gain energy, keep your skin glowing...the list goes on! If the headaches continue, use Basil in your food or simply sniff it. Don't ask!

Tomatoes

Another big moment after sniffing Basil, why don't you cut a tomato in slices, lay down and apply them on your face. Yes, you've heard me. Leave for 10-15 mns and rinse your face with warm water and dry gently. The acidity of the tomato will gently remove blackheads and leaves your skin clear and luminous. If any leftovers of basil and tomatoes, you may as well make some pasta!

Never underestimate

Who would think twice about Rosemary? Well, I wasn't until I realised this beautiful and tasty herb can make you a super hero with a clean liver on top. What is she on now?... you are thinking. Well, Rosemary can strengthen your adrenal system weakened by stress, help concentration and memory, keep your brain alert, increase creativity, lift mood and stimulate your mind. You are ready for anything now, aren't you? Bring it on.

Cinnamon

Chocolate is my passion however Cinnamon could be my lover. What on earth is she talking about? Well, Cinnamon cures so many things: from cold, toothache, bad breath, type 2 diabetes, digestive issues...and combined with honey, it can help with weight loss. It is also a high antioxidant. Last but not least, it is an insect repellent and that my dear, makes me fall in love with it. Pure and simple.

Colours

Lights and colours have an impact on your mood so be aware of the colours you are wearing. They do influence how you feel. Red, yellow, pink, orange boost your energy. Green, Lavender, blue are calming. Black or grey can bring you down.

Oils

Oils are the easiest way to awake your senses. Few drops of Lavender will bring you peace and relaxation whereas Peppermint drops in the ventilation system of your car will keep you alert during a long drive. Talking about senses, few drops of Yang Yang into your hand cream will make your hands velvety and more I'm sure as it is well-known as an aphrodisiac...I'm not responsible for what happens afterwards, you've been warned.

Liver

Often abused, the liver can easily be supported with fruits like berries and cherries or fresh vegetables like artichokes, broccoli, celery, fennel. Sprinkle it all with sunflower seeds, Turmeric, Ginger, Onion, Parsley, Garlic. Simple steps to a healthy and very grateful liver.

Computer

Most of us are surrounded by computers and other technology and it is important to neutralise negative Chi. You can use Tourmaline, Fluorite, Turquoise, Jasper, Amazonite, Aventurine, Sodalite...The choice is yours depending on which stone resonates with you particularly. Place it next to the computer or between yourself and the piece of technology. Also, protect yourself with Salt Crystals lamps which neutralize electro-magnetic pollution altogether. Plus they look beautiful!

Detox

I believe in gentle regular detox of the body instead of those drastic one off madness we can see around. As the body produces daily toxins then it seems logical to me to incorporate a variety of elements to support their elimination on a daily basis. Mix and match as you like so you don't get bored: eat black radish, onions, garlic, ginger, turmeric, lemon, artichokes, beets, asparagus, broccoli, avocado, cabbage, grapefruit, lemongrass, kale, seaweed, watercress, wheatgrass. You might not want to hear the eternal "drink water" however it works so add lemon may be, think outside the box and drink Dandelion tea, Fennel tea, Peppermint tea, it all counts as fluids. As I'm killing the party, I may as well finish it off: avoid alcohols, caffeine, sugar, chocolate, sweets, cakes for a little while or keep those as treats. You might find them too strong after a while actually or to the contrary, even more enjoyable. Everyone is a winner! I better run now....security, help!

Skin

Make up is for some a daily routine. Removing it should be done twice at night. You'll be surprised how much dirt is still present on your skin. Then spray some Rose water, let it dry naturally then do nothing. Yes, you heard me! Let your skin breathe. Make up, pollution, wind, harsh weather, central heating...your skin comes under continuous attack. Give it a break, let it do what it does naturally. It will probably feel weird at first but you will thank me later. You will glow. Drink water with lemon (magical potion) and plenty of Thyme tea. Feed it from the inside with butter (not cooked) and Olive oil to add to its elasticity. Sprinkle your food with Turmeric which will keep your skin clear and moisturized; reduce acne scars, blackheads, dark spots and eczema. Simple!

Rose water

The best well-kept secret in France until now...oh la la! I swear by it and won't go to bed without a spray of Rose Water on my face. For some, it is No5 and for others...water! Precious one though as it is anti-irritation, calming, anti-bacterial and wait for it, anti-ageing. Remove all make up twice, you'll be surprised and spray your face with Rose Water then let it dry naturally. It smells beautiful as well. I personally don't apply moisturizer at night and let my skin breathe. Soon, your skin will glow like never before. Yes!

Something to drink

Not again! Yes, but this time it is Nettle which works wonders for stress, depression, hair loss, anaemia, infections, stomach aches, cystitis, skin...and much more plus it is packed with Potassium, Manganese, Calcium, Iron, Vitamin A, C and B. Go on, on the house!

Hair

My hair doesn't stop to surprise me on a daily basis particularly when I wake up. Trust me, you better be ready for that. Forget about black coffee if you are hungover, just have a look at my hair and I guarantee you'll wake up...screaming! So, for those of you who want to add some shine to their hair, replace your shampoo with an egg and rinse presto with cold water otherwise sticky scrambled eggs anyone? For those with itchy scalp, mix sliced cucumber, yoghurt and honey then massage your scalp and leave it for 15 min then wash. And for everyone, nourish your hair from within with brown rice, oranges, yellow and dark green vegetables, salmon, beans, nuts, eggs, whole grain, oysters, carrots. As for my hair...we all live in hope!

Black Radish

We all know the pink one. Well, the black one is more challenging to find however its benefits are countless: it regenerates cells, stimulates bile production, purifies blood, eliminates toxins, reduces bloating and acid reflux. Rich in Vitamin C, it fights infection and radicals, works wonders on the liver and Thyroid, eases bronchitis, colds and flu. Wow! I'm speechless...enjoy as it won't last very long.

Daily

Commit yourself to do few minutes exercises every day: for example, 15 squats then the plank for 30 sec to a minute then the "chair" against the wall as long as you can then on all fours, flex one leg and kick up 30 times on each side. Few minutes daily will shape your butt and stomach in no time.

Echinacea

Well-known for boosting the immune system and to fight colds and flu, this little beauty is not appreciated as the perfect remedy to hay fever. Very often, the body "reads" pollens as bugs therefore it eliminates them through tears, sneeze and more. I personally take few drops in the morning mixed with a bit of warm water and in the evening if needed. Tablets are in my view less effective as they have to go through the digestive system. Now you can appreciate a picnic or a romantic date in the park without turning into an itchy creature. Nice!

Perfumes

They say a lot about you. Apple, jasmine, lavender, patchouli, vanilla, rose, yang yang say love. Almond, basil, honeysuckle, lemon, pine say money and success. Coconut, frankincense, lilac, sandalwood, violet say protection and harmony. Green tea, lavender, lemongrass, lotus, musk, valerian say inspiration and intuition. Cinnamon regroups ALL of them. Simple!

Coffee or tea anyone?

The choice is yours but did you know that white tea prevents obesity, contents fluoride, has higher level of anti-oxidants and may prevent some type of cancers as well as Type 1 diabetes and heart disease? Coffee may prevent Alzheimer, Type 2 diabetes, heart disease and protects the liver, increases memory and reaction times. It's not all good though as coffee raises cholesterol, can contain up to 1000 chemicals, reduces blood flow to the heart. As for tea, it can contain pesticides even if labelled as organic, raises blood pressure, can cause anxiety, contains Tannin therefore reduces absorption of iron which leads to anaemia and if mixed with milk, looses all its anti-cancerous qualities. Did I kill the party?

Good guys, bad guys?

Olive oil and butter have both amazing benefits: Extra virgin olive oil can help lowering cholesterol & blood pressure. It is a natural antioxidant. It can help preventing cancer and cognitive decline associated with aging. It is rich in Vitamin E. Butter on the other side is rich in Vitamins A (vision), E, D and K as well as minerals like manganese, zinc and selenium. It is also a great source of iodine which is crucial for Thyroid's functions. Rich in fatty acids, it supports the immune system fighting micro-organisms in the intestine. It helps with brain functions and healthy skin thanks to its Omega 3 and 6. In conclusion, have a bit of both. Balance is everything! Am I becoming sensible?...Miracles do happen!

Panda eyes

Did you know that slow elimination or over worked kidneys can be one of the reasons of dark circle around the eyes? Anaemia, heredity, lack of sleep, food allergy, stress can also be the cause. First, drink lots of water; eat more fruits particularly grapes and vegs; reduce caffeine; drink herbal teas like dandelion, nettle & ginger; eat more parsley, cranberry, lemon, pumpkin seeds; cut back on sodium and alcohol...and see the difference. Do massage gently around the eyes to help with blood circulation, water retention and lymph stagnation. And for pure vanity, let's use some thin slices of potatoes, wash them and leave them on your eyes for 15mins. You'll look rested and refreshed. Panda no more!

Eggs

Eggs are so superfood and they don't even know it! They help preventing eyes degeneration and lower the risk of cataracts. They contain high quality of proteins and essential amino acids. They help preventing blood clots, stroke, heart attacks and regulate the nervous system. They contain natural Vitamin D as well as Vitamin B12 (hair and nails). Some may say they raise cholesterol when others say the opposite. I guess it varies on how many a week you consume and if you fry them or boil them. The choice is yours. Bon appétit!

Cracked heels

This is generally due to extreme dryness as no oil glands are present there so moisturising is crucial. Make sure diabetes or thyroid issues are not the cause though. Here are some home remedies: first soak your feet for 10 minutes in warm water with lemon juice which dissolves dead/dry skin then scrub gently. Don't get over excited there as you could make your skin too delicate. Mix a spoonful of olive oil with few drops of lemon or lavender oil then massage your feet. Put some socks on so your feet retain all the benefits. I know... sexy however in few days, your heels will be as smooth as silk...and that's sexy!

Scrub

Remember to scrub weekly your face and body. Use fine brown sugar and go up from your toes to the face to support your lymphatic system and blood circulation. Please be gentle as your lymph is just under your skin. We want to encourage it, not traumatise it. Dead skin and toxins will be flushed out and you will be glowing. Your skin will be silky. I also like to dry scrub my body daily from the toes to the top before jumping into the shower. Velvety!

Vitamin D

We all know about the damage, the sun can have on our skin. However it also provides us with the precious Vitamin D, the so called "Sunshine Vitamin" which affects 2000 genes in our body. It helps with the absorption of Calcium and Phosphorus. It supports the immune system and helps with bones and teeth. Eating salmon, sardines, eggs, cod liver oil, raw mackerel, oysters, mushrooms, tofu and fortified cereals can help as well as 10 minutes a day outdoors. However once on holidays, we seem to go a bit insane and store Vitamin D like there's no tomorrow. The sun is responsible to 80% of skin ageing. Yes, EIGHTY per cent! You heard me. A tan lasts few weeks, wrinkles for a lifetime. Apology for the reality check but you know me, straight to the point when it needs to be said.

Mosquitoes

Olive oil or sunflower oil (2 tablespoons) mixed with 10-25 drops of the essential oil of your choice: cinnamon, eucalyptus, citronella, orange or rose geranium will make the most perfect and natural mosquitoes repellent. Rub or spray on your skin and store in a dark bottle away from heat or sunlight. Please avoid sensitive eyes area. Et voila! You will smell divine and stay mosquitoes free. Plus depending on the mix you choose, you might attract other creatures... Do keep me informed! Happy to be a bridesmaid anytime!

Heat is on

Heat causes the body to be easily dehydrated. Drinking water is one thing but eating food containing water can help. Oranges, grapefruits, pineapples, watermelons, broccoli, tomatoes contain up to 90% water. Yoghurts, cucumber, zucchini, radishes, salads, coconut water will also help you stay hydrated. Sea salts contain 84 minerals and nutrients therefore they will keep your energy going.

Au naturel

Be careful of wearing blush while in the sun. I have serious doubts. Talc, Silica, Alumina, Parabens are the common and yet toxic ingredients of blush. Iron oxides for colour and mica instead of talc are better options, it seems... What about wearing nothing but your beautiful self and let life make you blush when needed...I'm sure you see what I mean. I blush...yes I do. Give me a compliment and I'm like a tomato. Did I just beg for a compliment just there?...

Hands

Too often forgotten, our hands are giving us away. Those little dark spots often called age spots are generally due to sun exposure. Just as you apply sun protection to your face, do not forget your hands. Lemon juice, buttermilk, Tea Tree oil, Apple cider vinegar can help fade them away. Green papaya rub left for 20 min may help as well as raw garlic rub...Us French put garlic everywhere, don't we? We can't help ourselves!

Calcium

Many think Calcium is all about dairy products however they can be difficult to digest as an adult. As we know, Calcium helps maintaining strong bones and teeth, healthy blood vessels and could prevent insulin resistance. So indulge yourself on canned Sardines and Salmon as the Calcium is in the bones, White beans, dried Figs, Bok Choy, Kale, Black eye Peas, Almonds, Tahini, Orange, Sesame seeds, Seaweed, Instant Oats, Firm Tofu, Broccoli and Parsley. What a feast!

Nailed it

Let it free, let it free, let it free! A nail is a great indicator of our general health. If pale, it can be about ageing, anaemia, liver disease or malnutrition. If yellow, it can be fungal infection and more rarely, severe thyroid, diabetes or lung disease. Vertical ridges are usually harmless and simply caused by ageing. If horizontal, it may be an underlying condition so seek medical advice. Cracked or splitting nails are generally linked to thyroid condition. However we can't generalise so do not obsess about it. Let your nails breath once in a while, let them free.

Let's get nuts!

Mix and match Almonds for Calcium (bones) and Vitamin E (skin); Brazil nuts for Selenium (Thyroid and immunity); Cashews for Iron, Zinc and Magnesium; Hazelnuts for Homocysteine (heart); Macadamias for Calcium, Magnesium, Potassium; Pecan and Walnuts to help lowering cholesterol. So let's get crazy on nuts!...for those of you who still wonder, I'm already there!

Simple and effective

The "Frenchy me" will encourage you to add Mustard to your food as it stimulates the secretion of digestive juices and speeds up the whole process. Reducing the production of excess acid, you can now say "Au revoir" to this horrible feeling of heartburn. Another beauty is: Turmeric is a herbaceous plant very rich in anti-oxidants which works wonders with arthritis, infections, menstrual problems, digestion, liver disease, colds, bronchitis as well as slowing down the progression of debilitating diseases such as Alzheimer, depression and some will say helping fighting cancer. It's also called...are you ready for this? Curcuma Longa. How exotic! Et voila! Let's use food for pleasure and cure.

Winter time

Lower temperatures are no excuse to get into premature hibernation so let's get some energy flowing: do squats, plank, push ups, press ups...whatever it takes but keep moving. Keep the body tight. Then balance it out with a clear mind: stay put and let your thoughts pass by. Breathe. Hydrate in & out. Add fresh lemon juice, honey, ginger, garlic, onions, dark chocolate, nuts, seasonal fruits and green vegetables to your daily intake. Come on!

Cider

Some of us if not everyone might indulge themselves sometimes so drink 2 teaspoons of Apple Cider Vinegar in a bit of water...you'll get used to the taste eventually and trust me, it's worth it. From curing hiccups, soothing intestinal spasms, preventing indigestion to alleviating cold symptoms, clearing stuffy nose, it also helps fighting diabetes, heart problems, high cholesterol, weight issues, night time leg cramps. It helps rebalancing the body's pH helping it to detox. It can reduce heartburns, help getting rid of Candida (thrush, fatigue, poor memory, sugar cravings, yeast infections) and even whitening teeth. So what's not to like really?

Bubbles

My second passion after dark chocolate has to be Champagne! And guess what? it has health benefits...Yes it does. It may lower blood pressure and reduce the risk of stroke and heart disease. It contains high levels of polyphenols, a kind of antioxidant. It defends nerves from injury and boosts mood. Et voila! I knew it was good for me...

Thyme and thyme again

Thyme is my saviour and so, for many years. Not only does it work wonders for cough, colds and bronchitis but also for any digestives issues. It is also full of antioxidants and helps keeping your skin simply beautiful. It has antiseptic and anti-fungal qualities. It is rich in potassium, iron, calcium, manganese, magnesium and selenium, vitamins A, B6, C, E, K and folic acid. I usually drink it as a tea however you can use it in your cooking. Whatever rocks your boat!
Grow your own Thyme and use it as you feel. Be creative and simply enjoy!

Magnesium

It is an essential mineral involved in more than 300 biochemical reactions in the body. It regulates muscle and nerve functions as well as a healthy immune system & heart rhythm. It also helps building strong bones. If deficient in Magnesium: anxiety, migraines, high blood pressure, osteoporosis can occur to name a few. It can be found in dark leafy greens like Spinach and Kale; nuts and seeds like Almonds and Brazil nuts; fish like Mackerel or Tuna; beans and lentils; wholegrains like brown Rice; Avocadoes; low fat dairy like Goat cheese; Bananas; dried Figs; Tahini and more surprisingly Coriander, Dill and Sage. So no excuse to day dream about dark Chocolate...who am I kidding?

Camellia oil

It has been used for centuries in Japan on face, body, hair and nails. It is made from the extraction of Camellia flower seeds and is rich in vitamins A, B, C, E and Polyphenol, a natural antioxidant which protects from pollution and UV. It is full of essential fatty acid so the skin feels hydrated with a renewed elasticity. Quickly absorbed, the skin feels soft and non greasy. It helps with lines, wrinkles, the appearance of pores and stretch marks. It is of great help when exposed to air conditioning, sun or simply stressed and dehydrated. It works wonders as well on hair so massage your scalp before shampoo or add few drops on damp hair. Your hair will look healthy and shiny. Do not forget your hands and nails, they will be grateful. I use Organic Camellia oil when I give a Tsuboki Japanese facial massage. It simply works beautifully with the technique. The full experience is extremely relaxing with a gentle neck massage and acupressure on the face. It feels like a full body massage even though I only work on the face. The skin looks and feels hydrated. As one of my clients said: "You took years off me". What a nice feeling!

The beach

When the beach is getting closer, the concern is getting bigger...I'm obviously talking about water retention we might find on some parts of the body. That has to go and presto! Here are 5 steps for you to follow: 1) Dry scrub your body daily before your shower gently and upwards from ankles to shoulders. Keep it gentle as it is similar to a lymphatic massage and if you are too rough, you won't help the flow but interfere with it instead. 2) Drink Dandelion Tea as it helps cleansing the liver, bladder and kidneys; aids weight loss; provides brilliant vitamins and minerals. Taste wise...well, focus your attention on the beach! 3) Dehydration is bizarrely linked to water retention as the body seems to hold on to water in order to protect its vital tissues so eat regularly, drink water, avoid caffeine and alcohol, eat alkaline food. 4) Stop sugar. We all know it. Get your vitamins from vegetables instead of fruits for a while as too much fructose can be harmful as well as maintaining that sweet tooth of ours. 5) Plank, squats, the chair...the usual suspects. I know you love them. You are welcome. Anytime!

Almond
Almond milk keeps the heart healthy, the bones strong, the skin glowing, helps with muscles strength and healing, helps digestion as it contains fibre and it is obviously lactose free. I'm loving it! It contains Magnesium, Calcium, Copper, Zinc, Iron, Manganese, Phosphorus, Potassium and Selenium. Obviously not suitable for people suffering from nuts allergy.

Our little secret
Ladies, one part of our body we never work out even though it would need all our attention as it loses its tightness with time...it is, you've guessed it, our vagina. If there's one place we want to keep tight is that one so once again, there's no miracle: exercise is the answer. So while you are on the tube doing nothing, hold it tight as you would if you were trying to stop peeing and so, for 10 seconds then relax. Do this ten times twice a day. It will take a month but boy, it is worth it. Whether childbirth or not, this part requires attention so come on girls, squeeze! Plus, it is quite naughty to do this when nobody knows...cheeky! Your daily commute will never be the same.

We may as well
Once cheeky, always cheeky so let's carry on with some va va voom. Food you might like to bring into your diet to add some spice under the sheets or wherever...Asparagus (sorry), banana, almonds, oysters, chocolate (I knew it), honey, figs, garlic, basil, avocado. The rest is up to you!

Nectarines
Originally from China, they are rich in Beta-Carotene, a powerful antioxidant which turns into Vitamin A in the body therefore helps with bone development, reproductive disorders and keeps eyes healthy. They contain Vitamin C which protects the body from diseases, toxins and pollutants. They also are rich in Lutein which helps to keep eyes and skin healthy. They are full of Calcium, Magnesium, Iron, Folic Acid and

Vitamin K. They contain a great amount of Potassium which helps metabolism, regulates PH balance, helps digest carbohydrates and assists proteins synthesis. Plus their skin is softer than peaches which means I can eat them without having my mouth on fire...don't ask!

Citrine

Called the "Success stone", this joyful yellowish stone brings abundance & good luck in all areas. It lights up people's life. It brings success in business, cash flow as well as generosity so prosperity is shared. A solar plexus chakra stone magnifies personal power and energy. It helps fight negativity dissipating unwanted energy at home, office or car. It helps with family issues resolutions. As it doesn't absorb negative energy, it doesn't need energetic clearing. It brings stability and protection. It is useful for meditation and spiritual growth. It is the "happy stone" bringing confidence, creativity, honesty. It relieves fear of being alone or unworthy of love. It removes anger. It helps fighting depression and supports digestion, thyroid, sleep disturbances, muscles, kidneys, heart. It also removes toxins and overcomes addictions. I would call it "magic stone"!

Lines and wrinkles

The birth of a wrinkle is often due to the constant use of a network of muscles: we talk (I definitely do as you know...behave yourself!), sneeze, chew, smile, giggle (I do that too...a lot), yawn, laugh our head off and create tension and contraction of our muscles which naturally leads to a constriction of muscle tissue. The blood & lymph can't circulate and flow as usual therefore the facial tissue starts to die losing its elasticity. Wow! Did I just kill the party again? Do not despair, there's hope. Cold water on your face first thing in the morning will help with blood circulation. Rose water will slow down the ageing process, tighten pores and add glow to your skin. Drink lots of water. Eat avocados, nuts & seeds and let's not forget butter & olive oil. Moisturise in and out! Tsuboki Japanese facial massage can help the flow of energy through eight meridians, improve muscle tone and increase the flow of blood to the face. So let it glow, let it glow, let it glow!

Grapes

They are my cup of tea. What is she talking about now? ...no more wine for her! Grapes help with asthma increasing moisturise in the lungs, heart diseases, constipation, fatigue, indigestion, dental care preventing cavities, bones, diabetes, kidney disorders, cholesterol, Alzheimer, cataracts...They are full of antioxidants: copper, manganese, iron, potassium, magnesium, Vitamins C, B6, K, Riboflavin and Thiamin. Some will say grapes help preventing cancer and particularly breast cancer. I would suggest to follow the seasons and trust Nature as it knows best, giving us what we need when we need it. So we are clear, I suggest to eat more grapes and not drinking more wine. Just want to make sure we are on the same wave length...cheeky little monkey!

Not quite yourself

Feeling under the weather, uninspired and sluggish? Stop right there. I have the perfect solution for you. Walking is easy and manageable with no expense. It helps with body fat loss, engages and tones those challenging areas we all know: legs, bum and stomach. Let's not forget that swinging your arms will tone them as well as the upper back and shoulders. It boosts your Vitamin D and energy levels. Blood and lymph are gently massaged and more oxygen makes you feel more alive and positive. Exactly what we want. It releases endorphins and clear the mind. Feel good effect guaranteed! It reduces the risk of heart disease, stroke, diabetes, asthma. As it strengthens the density of the bones, it also reduces the risk of osteoporosis. It may reduce the risk of dementia by 40%. What's not to like? Come on, go out there!

Chia

Those tiny little seeds are quite impressive and well-known for their unbelievable protein content with no cholesterol. Those beauties also offer 18% of the recommended daily intake in Calcium helping with strong bones, teeth and preventing Osteoporosis. Rich in manganese, phosphorus, Omega 3 and fibre, Chia is all about the good stuff! It is also currently studied as a natural cure for type 2 Diabetes. Pretty good! Those seeds contain Tryptophan, an amino acid which regulates appetite, sleep and mood. Originally from South America, Chia was largely used by Aztecs and Mayans. And guess what? Chia is the ancient Mayan word for "strength"...Superfood indeed!

Second brain

Forget about superheroes, you and I have not one but two brains. Who knew? Our "second brain" contains around 500 million neurons and is situated between the oesophagus and the anus. And by the way, it could be the one we should blame for any cravings for crisps and chocolate! I knew I had nothing to do with that,...me, Miss dark chocolate! Our "second brain", the enteric nervous system (ENS) controls the digestion and senses any environmental threats. That "gut feeling" we all know so well and sometimes choose to disregard, is sent to the primary brain and influences our well-being. Super power we have! Also that "second brain" alerts the primary one if a virus or bug are present and as a result, vomiting or diarrhea happen as a defence mechanism. Too much information may be. Did you know that 95% of the body serotonin, the so called "feel good" molecule is in the second brain? Nerve signals sent from the gut towards the brain affect the mood so let's keep that gut healthy therefore happy! This simply reaffirms my view of the body in a holistic way as the branches of the same tree. Beautiful!

The Three Musketeers

Who would believe that my latest addiction is not chocolate but ...prepare yourself... black pepper, turmeric and cinnamon. What's happened to me? Those fight colds and flu; help with digestion& weight loss; clear the skin; are powerful antioxidants therefore anti-aging; fight candida, IBS, depression, tooth decay, PMS; prevent cancer, Alzheimer, Parkinson and taste amazing. Et voila!

Sugar

Let's get that straight: I might not become the most popular one in the next few seconds. OK, let's do this! Sugar is your worst enemy as it upsets hormone levels; it causes premature wrinkles by affecting the flexibility of proteins such as collagen and elastin; gives you a quick fix of energy then drains you down; it's highly addictive; it damages your teeth and gums; it feeds yeasts in your guts which disrupts your immune system; it makes you sweat in excess and with a heavy smell and talking about odours, it makes you break winds and it can lead to heart disease. I'm done with the good news so what are we going to do about this? Cut it out altogether for a while could be an option however it might be extreme for some so let's cut down gently on fruits as fructose is still sugar. Drink water with lemon when you feel like sugar. Go for a run and sweat it off. Support your system with Echinacea drops. Drink Aloe Vera first thing in the morning as it detoxifies the body, reduces unfriendly bacteria in the gut, helps healing gums, alkalizes the body reducing inflammation, works wonders for the skin, hair and nails and is a powerhouse of vitamins & minerals. You can do this.

Food for the heart

Let's keep that beautiful organ of yours in great shape with apples which will reduce blood clots thanks to its quercetin; avocados rich in antioxidants; green leafy vegetables & whole grains rich in vitamins, minerals and fibre; oats, walnuts & olive oil which help reducing cholesterol; red wine as it contains polyphenols (one glass a day... don't push it!); salmon rich in omega-3 fatty acids reducing inflammation, blood clots and cholesterol; soy protein which prevents heart attacks and tomatoes rich in lycopene which prevents heart diseases. All sorted now and ready to go!

Propolis

Bees are miracle-workers and produce honey, royal jelly, wax and propolis which are all good for our health helping with flu, cold, bronchitis, ulcers, headaches, infections within the intestines, cystitis, gums disease, blood circulation, arthritis..etc. Regarding propolis, it was used by Stradivarius himself to vanish the wood of his violins to protect them for years. Nothing has changed in the process as those beauties are still protected nowadays by what is called "the Russian vanish". Greeks used it for abscesses when Egyptians used it to embalm mummies. Not bad for an insect! So this ancient remedy helps boosting the immune system, improves skin and reduces breakouts, fights bacteria and fungi, lowers cholesterol, improves hair and nails' growth, increases vitality and productivity. A real miracle! The only warning would be though an allergy some people may have to honey so as a precaution, put some propolis on your forearm for few hours and test for any reactions. Otherwise, you are good to go!

Oregano

Oregano which means "Mountain Joy" and symbol of happiness for Greeks and Romans...not that you needed to know that...is an amazing anti-fungal, anti-bacterial, anti-inflammatory. Even "anti-bloating" so no wonder it brings joy and happiness to everyone! I need to grow up, I know!

Adrenals

When stressed and run down, our adrenals glands situated at the top of each kidney become overwhelmed. They help regulate our blood sugar levels and the balance between salt and water in our body as well as our sexual maturity. When under pressure physically and emotionally, our adrenals suffer and we can experience fatigue, inability to cope, dizziness and low stamina. So let's feed & support our adrenals with small and regular healthy snacks rich in Vitamin B which can be found in oats, Brazil nuts, bananas, legumes, potatoes, avocados, tuna, beef, turkey and tuna for example. As well as Vitamin C found in broccoli, Spring greens, Brussels sprouts, tomatoes, peaches, berries, mangoes, citrus fruits to name a few. Your adrenals will be grateful!

Happy cells

As one of my favourite writers Iyanla Vanzant says:"We are, to ourselves, the most valuable possession we have" so let's be gentle and nurture ourselves. When in panic and stress, let's breathe a few times and see what can be done right now instead. Get into action then trust life. Let life happen and unfold itself. Our mind can sometimes be over controlling. Life on the other hand is full of surprises: synchronicity works every time. Choose to pay attention to those little miracles. Be grateful for them and more will come, of course. At bed time, why don't you do this funny exercise? From toes to head (I prefer in that direction but feel free to do head to toes): thanks all the cells, organs, limbs, skin...etc of your body for supporting you all those years, for being so resilient and never letting you down. You will feel so alive and full of "happy cells" ready to serve you even more. A wonderful feeling, a vibrant energy filled with joy and serenity. Sweet dreams!

Eat seasonal

It would be expected from me to obsess about dark chocolate over Easter but I'm going to surprise you and talk about eating what is in season in this country. So in the UK: cabbage, cauliflower, celeriac...so far, not so good I guess but stay with me, it gets better... cod, crab, grapefruit, halibut, lamb, new potatoes, peas, lettuce, radish, rhubarb, salmon, spinach, Spring greens, watercress. I told you it was getting better! As for the readers living outside of the UK...do your homework. I'm outrageous, I know!

Tsuboki

Allow me to surprise you: did you know the large intestine is not only linked to the natural elimination process but also on an emotional level to the ability or not, to let go? The stomach as we know, starts to break down food but emotionally can be linked to over thinking, worrying, feeling anxious and unstable or self-pity. The small intestine is all about assimilation, separating the good nutrients to the "baddies" but emotionally, it is linked to poor judgment, inability to make decisions or someone being easily shocked. As for the bladder, it is emotionally linked to the inability to relax or being too timid. The gallbladder and liver are connected to indecision, being over worked, frustration, irritability and bitterness. The Governing Vessel is about lack of vitality and the Conception Vessel to lack of willpower. Is that fascinating or not? And that's what Tsuboki is all about. It's not just about prevention of lines and wrinkles or that beautiful glow, it goes much deeper. Magic!

Nails and Hair

Good hair day and strong nails make a big difference to the start of your day. As for mine, forget about the hair as it is more about managing those crazy curls than anything else and I put it nicely as I generally asked myself on a daily basis...what happened? And trust me nothing can explain that hair in the morning. So here are some keratin boosters for you: eggs which are very rich as well in Biotin or Vitamin B8; red meat which contains iron; blueberries which are among the strongest antioxidants and help as well with blood circulation; almonds as they are a source of proteins but also of magnesium (other sources: green vegetables, cocoa..); beer as it contains silica and helps with circulation; oysters as they contain zinc which can explain those white spots on nails if you are deficient; Vitamin D makes a huge difference in helping "fixing" vitamins and minerals in the body; salmon helps with reducing inflammation and is rich in biotin & omega 3; nettle works wonders as it is full of vitamins and minerals so feel free to boil some fresh leaves (good luck with picking them up...it is worth it so go on), let it rest, mix it with a glass of cider vinegar, add few drops of grapefruit essential oil then massage your scalp, you'll be amazed. I wonder if that could work on my crazy morning curls...

Green clay

One little secret after another! Us French use Rose water on our skin...I've bored you to death about it however did I tell you about the Green French

Clay and its amazing benefits whether as an internal or external use? This very fine clay is negatively charged therefore it "attracts" positively charged toxins, acidic residues and other baddies which are then flushed away. All you have to do is to put one tablespoon of clay in a glass of water overnight and drink the water in the morning as all the clay will be resting at the bottom of the glass. Do this for a week and your colon & intestine will be de-toxed; your immune system will be boosted as clay is very rich in vitamins and minerals...Also, let's not forget it can be used externally as a mask and will unclog and shrink the pores as well as brighten your skin without drying it. Clay can even help with sun burn, eczema, acne and even toothache. What a magnificent natural product! I like simplicity as you know and this is music to my ears. Can't be too French....sometimes!

Small yet powerful

Here is something that completely fascinates me! Nothing to do with chocolates, dogs or that mysterious someone. I'm talking about the one and only Amygdala. That little wonder in the shape of an almond in our brain is responsible for the perception and process of our emotions, the control of aggression as well as our libido. That mysterious someone might be involved in this after all...the suspense is unbearable, don't you think? Back to Amygdala now: it is so little yet powerful as it is responsible in determining which memory is stored therefore our emotional response to an event linked to a past event will be defined by it. This is huge. EFT also called tapping is very much based on this and allows people suffering from traumas, fear and pain to be free from those. The body and mind are simply the most incredible creation in this world and we are fortunate enough to live in one of those. Lucky us! So let's keep our beautiful mind and body in good shape as we are the humble guardians of this magnificent beauty!

MIND & SPIRIT

Procrastination is over

Our mind is so clever, it can justify almost anything. Particularly when we want to find excuses for not doing what we are supposed to do...and we might even blame others. Procrastination is a source of stress for many. Not anymore! Let's take responsibility here & now:

-make a list tonight of what you need to do tomorrow so your mind will have time to work on it & digest it overnight. Those are your intentions.

-break down big goals into smaller ones. And as you achieve the "baby steps", your self-confidence will grow dramatically.

-have deadlines and you'll surprise yourself achieving them. I know the rebel in you doesn't do deadlines...Are you afraid of a challenge?

-listen to what you say. Ban words like "but" from your vocabulary. It's like a brick wall. Replace it by "however" and the door of opportunities will open in front of you. Try those few tips and let's see what happens.

Daily adventure

Life is a daily experience so dare to step away from what you know. Open up to the unknown. It does take courage to do this as so many prefer to stay stuck and whine about it. Try something new today. Embrace the natural flow of life. Shut down the constant "blabla", the eternal inner judgement of the mind and let life surprise you. Blossom with excitement. Find your own truth, no right or wrong here, just yours. Embrace what you feel right now and see where it takes you.

Gratitude

Be grateful for those little things that come your way: your train came as you were entering the station; you got the last Mozzarella sandwich, your favourite...etc. Say thank you and see more wonders come your way. Remember your mind creates your reality, it's all energy. Your mind is a "happiness factory", use it. It's yours! Appreciate today in order to extend your joy into tomorrow. Thanks the Universe, God, your Highest Consciousness...whoever you feel more comfortable with and maintain this positive wave of energy into the next day. Be appreciative of what you have instead of focusing on what you lack. Immersed into this bath of gratitude, you will expand it wherever you go, whatever you do.

Harmony

For more harmony at home: hang some white garlic (French touch...couldn't help myself!) with a yellow ribbon or some lavender...probably smells better! However, you will feel the change in energy almost straight away. May be expand this to the office...just saying!

Money

Be grateful of all that abundance already around you will bring more abundance with money. Few things can also help: wear a Mother of Pearl stone; keep a Citrine in your purse; have a Money plant or Jade plant in your home; place a Basil plant near your front door. Stop focusing on the lack of it as what you focus on, you will attract more of it. Of course, you are aware of it however focus on solutions, practicalities, opportunities. Also clear your home will help clearing your mind and will bring that fresh start in your life. Plus you might find things to sell or to give to charity. Money is energy. Move it!

Healing

Forget about those who, without knowing you, put a label on you instead of looking within themselves. It is a reflexion on them and has nothing to do with you. Don't let those beings make you doubt of who you are and what you are capable of. You are bigger than that. Saying that, there's a part of you that hasn't been healed and this kind of situations brings it all back up. What would you say to a little child under such unfair treatment? Then comfort that little child who's been hurt. How does it feel to be looked after? Your healing process has just started. Simple and effective. Give yourself what others didn't and see your wounds heal. Don't let the past compromise today. Often, those situations come up in order to be shifted. Nice work!

Clarity

You are the centre of your Universe: be clear of what you are all about. In doubt, ask your friends and family. What were you like as a child, it might not be so far to who you are today! Be clear on what you want and the how will come. Be clear on what you won't compromise with. Your values are the very essence of yourself.

No pressure

Stay away from judgement. Who made us think we have to get it right all the time? The media, our education...whatever it is, it is a lot of rubbish. There's no right or wrong, just different routes which will get you to your destiny no matter what. So remove the pressure and enjoy the journey. You might see much more clearly what the next step is. See new opportunity presents itself which is much more exciting than to have it right. Stay present.

Surf life

Everything and everyone are in constant transformation. What seems negative now will soon transform in positive. It's just a matter of time. Nothing stays the same forever. The mind might judge this as scary and might attempt to control but it is not possible to control Life. So let it go, let it be. Live in peace with your surrounding. Do what needs to be done, keep your senses switch on and surf the waves of life.

Vibrations

Words are vibrations, they are energy so stay aware of the message you are literally sending to the Universe as it generally answers straight back. Choose your words carefully, take your time and show discipline. Accentuate on the positive and see the change in your life. Magical! Same things for thoughts. Only allow positive ones into your brain. Treat your mind as a freshly turned over soil. Only plant good seeds and not weeds. Then let nature do its magic and see beauty blossom all around you.

Clear up

De-clutter your home, desk, inbox, FB so-called "friends" and see your mind relax and at peace, ready to embrace a new space full of possibilities. That freshly clean sheet feeling!

Truth

Stay true to yourself. Choose to be who you really are and not waste time pleasing others, saying yes when you want to say no. Life is too short. Also, by projecting an image of someone who is not you, you end up attracting people who are not suitable to the real you. What a waste of time! What a waste of your life! This life is YOURS.

Guilt and regrets

No point living in the past with the weight of guilt and regrets. The "what ifs" and "if onlys" won't make any difference in your here & now. They are just slowing you down. They work hand in hand with procrastination. The point of the past is: good memories and lessons learned from the bad ones. That's it. So, be present in the here & now and you won't create more guilt and regrets for the future.

Listen

Cultivate stillness. Listen within and simply "check in": how are you feeling right now? Experience it instead of suppressing it so whatever it is, it will be released. Facing it instead of running away from it will make you grow stronger and shift quicker.

Why

Let's be honest: those eternal Monday's new beginnings rarely last passed Wednesday: exercise, diet, stop smoking...etc. The "usual suspects" (should, must, have to) come from the mind and not from our Truth therefore they rarely last. Knowing the WHY is more powerful and will keep us in flow where everything is effortless. Let's take a passion for example, turned into a business. There will be tough days however knowing why we chose to do it in the first place, what it brings into our life, the lifestyle & the freedom we can have will make those days easier and get the job done. Stick to your WHY and get lasting results.

Forgive

Forgive yourself and others. Set that intention, the how will come. Free yourself to that weight and fly high. Too many of us carry that invisible yet ferocious guilt or anger keeping us stuck. Stop punishing yourself. Free yourself instead. You are an intention away from freedom. That's all it takes, that first step. Go on!

Love

As the trunk of a tree, love stays strong and grounded. It's the constant element of Life. The world passes by, comes and goes. Its branches curve like a reed in the wind but love remains strong. A tree called Love.

Happy

You are running around between the children, partner, job, friends, keeping the household together...etc. Those are "happy problems". Yes, you have children and a home to look after...Yes, you have a partner to nag or who nags you... Yes, you have a job to moan about... Those are blessings. Many would wish to have those. Those "happy problems" which you will regret once they are gone; when the children are all grown up and have left home or a partner who'll never come back. We all have good days and bad days however take a minute, breathe deeply, prioritise and enjoy the rest of it.

Morning fog

Keep a pad and a pen next to your bed and write the first word or sentence that comes to you in the morning when your mind is not completely awake, not judging or "filtering" just yet your subconscious. Read it a week later, you might be surprised.

Egg & pyramid

How those two got together? You don't want to know. When you have a challenging day ahead: put yourself in an imaginary egg or pyramid. The egg can be golden and shinny and the pyramid covered with mirrors reflecting back the negativity to those with bad intentions...we all know who those are. Comes the end of the day, dissolve that vision into light. Sleep peacefully now.

Grounded and refreshed

Sit on a chair and grow some imaginary roots under your feet as big as the house you are in. Let them grow to the centre of the Earth, you may as well. Feel a white light from above your head and feel it "showering" you with its energy removing any negativity from you. You'll soon feel refreshed, grounded and protected.

Spirituality

Many of us prefer spirituality to religion. Taking some time out even for few minutes during the day and stay in silence; showing gratitude for the achievements & blessings of the day; keeping a diary; setting some intentions for tomorrow; keeping positive affirmations in mind or motivation...whatever works for you. Sprinkle your life with those gems so life is not uni-dimensional and not limited to work, eat and sleep. You are bigger than this. Mind, body, soul and so much more.

Power

You've made some decisions or strong resolutions, time to get into action. Why not wear Black Onyx or Tiger's Eye stones in order to enhance your willpower, courage and confidence? Come on champion, the sky is the limit!

Expectations

Expectations are like putting a frame around your life. You are limiting the potential of life. You stay stuck in one perspective and one only when life has so much more to offer. Doing something because we want to without expecting anything in return is one of the best sensations in the world. Giving and helping are simply magical. Don't get me wrong, it is also good to be ambitious and expect results but being driven shouldn't mean being side-blinded by it. As good as it can be to have a plan, stay in flow, open to the surprises of life. They could be better than your wilder dream. Step out of the frame!

First step

We all suffer from the "over thinking" syndrome. I have to say that my best decisions are probably the ones I just made on the spot. I obviously wouldn't advise this as a rule however over thinking life is not living it. Take a first step, today. Now. Just do it. It doesn't have to be huge, just a baby step. Make a list for example but don't become the "eternal list maker" neither, another syndrome we all know. Make a vision board, use visualisation and work backward to what would be the first step. May be ask around if someone knows a bit more about your idea, get some information, go online, find a group of like-minded people, go to network events. Go at your pace but go. Don't judge yourself for not doing enough though as it will result to a "oh well, why bother?" moment and we'll be back to square one, to procrastination and still there in a year time so go on, one step!

Treat

Why wait for a birthday or a new job to treat yourself? Why don't you go on a weekly date with yourself and treat yourself with some flowers, a new scarf or a nice walk in a beautiful park, go to a gallery and let your senses receive love and care. You deserve it. Plus there shouldn't be any disagreement between you and yourself then again...

Smell

Smell is the first sense to be developed as a human being. A smell can transport you to a different world altogether: the cakes, pasta cheese beignets and coffee mixed with chicory of my Grandmother; the wood in the fireplace; the air in the Pyrenees; my first perfume when I was thirteen; the smell of my nephews when they were babies; my Sister favourite perfume..etc. Use your special ones to change your reality whenever you are stuck in traffic or on the tube or simply in need of a break. A great and cheap way to travel the world and time. Bon voyage!

Don't be shy!

If you are like me and scare the birds when you sing then we should become a duet. What I'm trying to say is we tend to become more self-conscious as we get older. Well, it's more about health and safety in my case as I would probably scare the children too however I do not despair. So I tend to sing when I walk home from the station at night when my voice is covered by the traffic and very few people can see me. Yes, I'm going under cover. How refreshing and liberating it is to sing, I love it. When was the last time you did sing? Obviously if you meet me in the street at night, just ignore me...for your own sake.

Little puppy

The mind has a mind of itself and like with a young puppy, you have to show who's the boss here. Stay in the here and now, show discipline and awareness. When it starts wandering, bring it back to reality. Focus on your body, forget about judgement, see what is around you right now. Over-thinking can be worse than not thinking enough. Keep that little puppy under control.

Be proud

We've all heard of the gratitude list keeping our mind in a positive energy therefore creating more of it. Why about listing everything we've achieved to this day? I'm sure there's plenty. Quite often during an off day, we seem to forget our qualities, our resilience, our strength...Let's remind ourselves that despite what we've been through, we are still standing. Let's be proud of ourselves and trust that life only gives us what we can handle. We have what it takes to conquer it all. Life often "stretches" our muscles in more way than one, just to prove to us we can do it. So why do we doubt? Life doesn't.

Holidays

We all like a little break away from the routine, don't we? But why not integrate holidays elements within our daily life? Sitting on a terrace and take the time for a coffee full of aroma which transports you right back where you were instead of a take away coffee you will drink on your desk checking your emails. Taking a course and bake your own bread or prepare sushi, whatever rings your bell. Making your own perfume and soon integrate all those beautiful smells from your holidays into a bottle...Go on, break free and live on holidays all year around.

Silence

Daily moments of silence are priceless in the busy life we all lead in order to recharge batteries and give to our brain a well-deserved break. Everything seems "on the go" nowadays so make sure to find a precious moment of silence in your day, few minutes of inner peace. I like to "listen" to silence first thing in the morning when people sleep. It's magical as it is so rare. Just listen and do nothing! It will clear your mind, calm your body and recharge your soul.

Action

Action talks louder than words. So many words, so little done. Listen to the words however watch the action. Soon you will see the truth. As for yourself, here's an action booster: write down your goals with a deadline otherwise we'll spend Christmas over this. Writing brings clarity and deadline a kick in the "derriere". So it's not in your head anymore, it's already part of reality...I'm talking of your goal, not of the kick obviously or do I? When you write, you can see it, name it, you can hear yourself reading it. Your senses are awake and ready to go. It works!

VIPs

A wonderful way to count your blessings: get yourself a frame and fill it with the pictures of the core people of your life, the VIPs of your heart. Appreciate the diversity of your friends and family, the amount of people who love you back. You are so blessed as they are to have you in their life. YES!

Challenge

Stretch yourself with something different, something you are not good at, something completely alien to yourself as it will require all your attention therefore you will forget the stress of the day. Why not try ballet, rock climbing, belly dancing, knitting, Sushi making...etc. Something manual for those who are not, something active for those who are not, just challenge yourself and see the stress disappears. And as you give yourself a break, solutions may appear just like that!

I am...

Then fill in the rest as fast as you can. See what you come up with. What defines you today, most days, as a child...have you really changed that much in your core? You already knew then and you know today. Yes, you do. When you stop judging yourself which is very often the judgement someone else gave you then you will hear that well-hidden yet powerful voice of YOURSELF. Also fun to do: I like, I want, I love, I wish, I dream, I forgive. Don't over think it, just do it. Complete those as a game. You might surprise yourself.

Meditation made easy

Sitting on the bus, tube or simply laying down in the park, simply breathe in and say mentally "relax" and as you breathe out, say mentally "let go". Make sure you exhale it all and do not put pressure when you inhale as it is after all a natural reflex of ours in order to breathe.

Fly

We've all been hurt before however it's not a reason to close ourselves up, to not love anymore so stretch your wings slowly and gently, take a first step, remember who you are, how beautiful you are and fly again. Bon voyage!

Three

After a busy and probably stressful day, why don't you lay down next to your partner and name the best three events of the day ...instead of moaning and "catching" each other negativity? What happens next and particularly nine months later is not my fault. I just said lay down, nothing else, ok?

Now

Remember, there's always a solution whatever the situation is. Nothing lasts forever so know that this current situation will be over soon as Life is always transforming and moving forward. Instead of being in the fear and stress, focus on what can be done now. Ideas and opportunities will present themselves, this is Life, always in movement. Stay open. Remember how it happened before so it will happen again.

Stand

Stand up for who you are, for your beliefs and do not switch off your essence by fear or false excuses to keep the peace. Express yourself honestly. Reclaim your voice. Be proud of who you are, nobody can take that away from you. Stand up, stand out.

Pressure anyone?

Under stress, most of us panic. That's the trap. Do the complete opposite: take a break, breath, notice the tensions in your body and breath through them, drink water, eat something. This will allow you to come back to the "here and now" where all new opportunities present themselves. You can then pick and choose, prioritise, take baby steps and solve all issues one by one. Remember to maintain your sugar level as well as hydration in your body for a clearer mind. Nothing can stop you now!

Remedies

The usual suspects are generally fears, anxiety, doubts, worries and guilt. So the best remedies are doing, living, moving, laughing, meditating, loving. Don't switch off Life, keep your senses in awareness. Wake them up!

In & out

Inner peace will always reflect itself on your outer beauty. No expensive creams will ever erase someone's inner conflicts. Good genes, good diet, no smoking and low exposure to the sun might help however unresolved issues will "scar" your face and body. So get a good look at yourself in & out and face what's needed. You are beautiful!

In...deed

A good deed a day is something you probably already do without noticing however let's sprinkle an extra magic to people with a smile, a helping hand to someone in need, a shoulder for someone to rest on and cry or simply be next to someone so they never feel alone.

Ready steady go

Whatever you want to achieve, just start and see where it takes you: move energy, plant seeds, make a list, ask for information, email, call...it will all take you where you need to be. That's flow for you so just start.

Contrast

If you are unsure on what you want, make a list of everything you do not want anymore in your life. In this way, you will be able to see clearly your old habits like trying to please everyone, not saying no, forgetting your own goals and dreams...Sometimes it is easier to name and shame those ones however you will appreciate by contrast what you are looking for, what you are craving for. Whatever works!

Stay open

Don't be afraid of saying how much you love somebody. Many ways to do so: be tactile, hug, kiss, be thoughtful, listen, take time to share...Keep your heart opened despite having been hurt in the past, stay fresh. Life is too short and love precious. Stay open to love, you are worthy of it. Hurry to forgive, you will move faster in life and feel so much lighter. Stop punishing yourself by carrying what doesn't belong to you. Travel light. Spring clean your heart, remove old aches and pains. Make that decision, the "how" will come. Simply decide now.

Fun

Say yes to fun and laughter. Grab any opportunity for it, don't even think twice, just do it! We tend to make it far too complicated as we grow older...Aren't we supposed to grow wiser? Children know better. Time to giggle everyone! As if nobody watches you: dance, dance and dance! And if people see you, they can always join in! Embrace the freedom of the moment. Dance like there's no tomorrow. Free your body, release all tensions and before you know, you will have a smile on your face. Shake that butty of yours! YEAH, party time!

Perspective

There's a big picture out there. Name it as you like as we don't see it but know and trust that it will all work out for the best. Remind yourself of this particularly when things don't go well and panic shows up. Like a rubber band, stretch our mind and then let go. A gymnastic of the Soul! Do what you have to do, the "day to day" then let the magic happen. Allow it. Trust.

Rise

Remember that in any relationship, the other one is also on his/her journey. Simply concentrate on yours and grow. Forget about judgement, your time is better spent on your own process than speculation, expectation or anger. Rise and move forward!

Perfection

Perfection is all around you and within as well. Trust all is well and what needs to be sorted will be eventually. Give yourself more credit. "Everything is going to be alright" was what your parents /teachers were telling you when you fell down. You always got up and carried on. Nothing has changed. You are stronger than you think.

Check up

Check up with yourself on a daily basis. Keep a level of self-awareness. Easier to say than to do I agree however simple things help like daily writing, deep breathing, daily conscious walk, sit alone in silence, lay on the floor and close your eyes...It requires very little discipline however makes an enormous difference in your mood, focus, balance and well-being. Cherish that moment with yourself! A daily "rendez-vous". Not to be missed.

Friends

Brothers and sisters of the heart are your friends. Those special people who nurture you, challenge you, love you no matter what and never judge you. They make you grow, they feed you with their love and care, they are always there. May I salute you Angels of my heart for believing in me whatever I choose to do. I love you deeply. Call yours and tell them how you feel. Be there for them, cherish them, they are rare therefore precious.

Just do it

The perfect scenario rarely presents itself or what we judge as perfect...so don't wait for it before you get into action. Just do it. Dare. Start now. A small step might take you a long way. It all starts by one step like when you did walk for the very first time...Know what you believe in and start make it happen NOW! If it is in your mind, you know it is possible. And if it hasn't be done before, it is even better, be a pioneer. Just go for it!

Boomerang

Be aware of your words. Don't waste them for a start. Choose them carefully as they are filled with energy/vibration for others as well as yourself. They define your being now and in the future. Words can hurt and stay in your heart for a long time as well as they can help and heal just as much. Choose positive ones and see your world change. Try and see what happens. Enjoy!

Emotions

Allowing emotions to the surface is the first step to release them. Suppressing them will make them worse. They will build up and come out at the worst time possible. So choose a safe way to express them: write, dance, sing, watch a sad movie with chocolates (you know how much I love them, they are the answer to many ailments because of the Magnesium they contain....of course!). Whatever works for you, find a way to release them for your own good. Don't let them drive your life. It's your life, nobody else's.

Magic

Believe in magic! We grew up surrounded by fairytales and saw miracles in everything. That was our daily routine. When did we stop believe in miracles? Our mind is limiting us to what is possible....Boring! Let life take over and surprise you. The mind is small compare to your life force. Remember last time you fell in love, your mind had nothing to do with it. It was just magical! Believe in magic and see it happen AGAIN!

Wasted

Time is wasted every day with inner doubt, fear and limitation. So there's a cure for that: wear an elastic band on your wrist and pull it every time you find yourself in that mindset and believe you me, you will soon stop wasting your time. So if I come across people with a bruised wrist, I'll know you are on the road of full potential and joy. Just believe!

Expand

Something new every day is what you want: I'm not talking about a new pair of shoes...nice try! Whether it is a different route to go to work or build your new website yourself. Do something you've never done before, something you find difficult that makes your hands sweat (sexy I know) and your heart race. Just do it. And please start this on a Monday so you are set for a week of great achievements, breaking one boundary after another. Come on boys and girls!

Reset

Once you give your heart away, you rarely have it back in the same state. Whether it is not in one piece or it is bigger than ever, it is still YOURS. So re-set it from the start, remember your values, reconnect with your core, stay true to yourself and let life do the rest. Be pride of who you are. You are beautiful.

Rescue

Tempting as it can be, becoming the "plaster" of somebody else's heart, life, situation won't help neither them nor us. Being there and listening are often enough. They have to figure it out by themselves in order to learn. Rescuing others because we are too scared of dealing with our own issues is not serving anyone. Ouch!... Let's be strong. We can do this!

Kindness

So often, we are judging ourselves and others. Let's appreciate that the five fingers of one hand are from the same being and yet very different. We might have our very unique identity, thoughts and ways of doing things however we all belong to the same source. Let's be kind to each other!

Emotional detox

Often a detox is all about a physical cleansing, an elimination of toxins. What about an emotional one? A good clear-up of old thoughts, feelings, regrets which we are carrying around...for nothing! Time to detox: write religiously everyday and let your thoughts wander, ask questions, write them down and see the magic happen. And guess what? I wouldn't be surprised those extra pounds/kilos vanish for good. You bet?

Trust

Trust is different than belief. Trust is our inner connection to the Truth. We just know. Belief on the other hand is very often the by-product of our programming whether it is from education, religion, society..etc. Just clear yourself from it and go to your core. You know what is good for you. You just do.

Check in

By asking yourself this simple question: is this right for me now? You will be aware of the now and focus on you. By checking in within yourself, you will stay on the right trajectory and shine your light to the world. Yes!

Magic formula

Simply ask and allow yourself to receive. By asking, you become clearer on your intentions. By allowing, you trust the Universe to provide as It always did and always will do. More importantly, you open up your heart. And when this door is opened, there's no limit to the gifts of life. Plenty to come, I promise!

Choice

Life is not determined by our situation, our past, our gender, our culture...etc, it is determined by our decisions today. The past is behind us, no need to dwell on it. Make that choice now: who do you want to be? What do you want? What can you do now? And do something about it. Then "float" with the Universe, abandon yourself to the flow of life. Taste something different NOW and be amazed!

Body

Let's be grateful for our magnificent body which works magic every single second of our life, for the roof over our head, for the food on our table, for the people we have in our life, for the love we have to give and for the one we receive. We are so blessed. Let's take a moment to appreciate. Let's not forget how privileged we are.

Pack

The question is: what is it you need to improve in your life/body/work? What are you procrastinating about? Keep asking questions. Be brutally honest then take action. The secret is to make a pack with a friend. Shake hands on it. Commit to it. Your friends are your mentors. They love you enough to tell you the truth no matter what. Or come and see me and I shall tell you... gently but truly. You know I will.

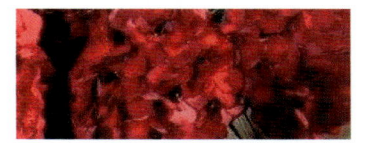

Full Moon

At that time, there's a lot of movement around: oceans get affected, animals react differently, many babies are born on that night...Electricity can be felt in the air as well. Use that amazing energy in a constructive way and "give birth" to whatever you have in mind. Take a moment to feel its grounding power. It's so much bigger than us. Have a moon bath, clothes on or not...your call!

Words

Some choose to surround themselves with powerful words or sentences around the house, on their desk, on their mobile. Choose them carefully. They are filled with energy and can motivate you, uplift you or its contrary. What is the first word that comes to your mind? Play with it!

Simple

Urban life makes us forget this simple truth: "No matter what, plants keep growing, reaching for the light, feeding themselves with what they need". A beautiful reminder from a wise Chinese lady in a garden centre last week...Read it literally or not. Food for thought or simply nurturing yourself, the choice is yours!

Spinning

When the mind is busy, keep the body active. In Metamorphic Technique, we work with the 3 centres: moving (feet) doing (hands) thinking (head). And we want them to be balanced. So if your head is spinning, go for a walk or start knitting or baking and your thoughts will fall into place. If not, come and see me!

Starting blocks

Start your day by setting an intention, being grateful, acting as if it already happened, surrendering then staying silent for few minutes. See the magic happens.

Change something today!

Let's not get stuck in our routine: eat something you never tried before, experiment. Think differently about someone and see how everything else transforms. Put a different rainbow of colours in your everyday life. That simple conscious decision can change the rest of your life. It all starts with a thought. Simple energy/vibration changes the whole perspective. Have fun with it!

Now

Too often the fear of failure stops us from doing something. "Worry is a pray for negativity" as we all know. So jump in, challenge yourself. Stop thinking and start doing. We are all children in need of approval of some sort however remember you are the only one living your life. You are not here to nourish anyone's expectations, not even yours. So go for it NOW!

Face it

The best way to stay true to yourself is to bare it all. Remove all "make up", have a good look in the mirror, assess the situation and take the necessary action here and then. No messing around. Time to do things differently. Or guess what? You'll be in the same place next year! Time to move forward.

Seasons

There are seasons in life: one to blossom, one to cultivate, one to plant, one to rest. Allow yourself to go through them. You can't force Nature so be kind to yourself and follow your inner rhythm. Each season brings its own lessons. Enjoy!

Wave

Sometimes the deepest shifts feel like a slow wave. Reaching deeper, it takes you further and reaches higher peaks. Stay with the flow, surf on the wave. Surrender and enjoy the ride! Life is good.

Be

When the mind is foggy, when you can't think straight...you actually have the opportunity to just BE. Give yourself permission to do just that. You don't need to get it all figured out. Be kind to yourself.

Dream big

Be clear on what you want, your goals and intentions. The "how" will come to you, don't worry. Just see your dream, feel it, smell it. Know what you want. Wishing for it is not strong enough, WANT it. Then show up with Life. Say yes and see the magic happens. You were born for happiness then got "polluted or distracted" by others' fears. Allow happiness to come back to you, you deserve it. Break free from limitations that don't belong to you. Stay magical!

Sweat it off!

Not talking about the excess of food and alcohol but more about the emotions which you've been carrying for far too long. Time to let go. Time to travel light, don't you think? Write them down, talk them through, cry them all...whatever works. Make sure you go to the core. Listen to your body. What do you feel and where? then ask questions. Why? That's a good one and see what comes up. Shift the unnecessary. Time to fly high, time to fly light!

Giving

"We make a living by what we get, we make a life by what we give." Wilson Churchill. Isn't it true that what we give brings us a sense of purpose? Coming from the heart brings peace and removes guilt. It makes the journey simpler and clearer. Following the heart brings no regret, it simply creates memories. What do you think?

Voice it

Whatever you are feeling, give it a voice. Do not try to control it all otherwise the emotion will build up. Experience the emotion, voice it then you will be able to release it. Smiling when you want to cry or simply "pushing it under the carpet" will make it worse. Find a healthy and safe way to express it: sing, talk to someone you trust, go for a walk to clear your mind, cry or laugh, draw, paint...whatever it takes for you not to carry that extra bag you don't need.

As you are

Be your own best friend, love yourself right where you are and the way you want someone to love you.

True colours

Someone with walls all around himself or herself is not that strong. If he/she was, there would be no more mask, only true colours, straight to the point opinions and real actions. Be true, be strong!

Naturally

Showing up in life is crucial. Stretch yourself, take on a new challenge. Action combined with courage are unstoppable. Be clear and specific on what you want, stay practical and the how will come naturally.

Miracles

They are possible, they happen all the time. We just take them for granted. Our body is a miracle and continues to be every instant. Believe! We don't have to figure everything out.

Scared

Are you scared to be happy? What would that mean to you? What would change in your life that you are not ready to let go just yet? Just wondering.

Beliefs

Challenge your beliefs, they don't belong to you most of the time and guess what, they are just beliefs, a thought which was repeated far too many times. You can do anything. Limitation is a belief as non-limitation. Which one do you want to take on?

Simple question

How do you see yourself? The answer might explain your current reality.

Just take a moment and describe yourself as you would do about somebody else. Might feel weird at first but carry on. Your choice of words, lack of them, intonation...might give you the answer you've been looking for.

Bruised

The bruises of the heart take longer to heal. Nurture yourself. Be gentle with yourself. Don't push. They will pass.

Precious

Fifty per cent of our time is lost in thoughts. The present moment is so underrated. Show up!

Special

When someone opens up, it is so courageous and powerful. Appreciate it. Life might be busy however let's stop and share this together.

Yes

Stop judging yourself and see how things become easier suddenly.

Then treat yourself every week: a film, flowers, lingerie, treatment, time with friends, a nice walk, good food... You deserve it. Go out there and play. Life is good!

Decide

Decide to be successful. Decide to be happy. You heard me: DECIDE. This word means "cut off" in Latin root. Cut off any other options and become unstoppable. No plan B. Come on!

What

What is your magic? What is your talent? What are you the best at? If you don't know, ask friends and family. That's your magic. Now, it's your duty to spread it to the world. Guess what? As you do this, it won't feel like work and success will simply happen.

Wealth

Wealth is not just about money, it's more than that. Why not make a list of "wealth gratitude", a list of everything you are already rich of? friends, love, health, a place you can call home, food, work, passion, projects...Then "bathing" in that sea of gratitude, let the magic happen and see more of the good stuff coming your way. Enjoy! One thing though, you are always richer for how much you give.

Free

Always remember you are a free spirit: nothing, no one can take that away from you. You are your own being no matter what.

Process

Trust the process. Whatever you believe in or not, trust you are in the right place at the right time. It removes a lot of anxiety by giving the mind and the ego something to "chew" on freeing energy to simply be present and grab opportunities in the here & now.

Notice

What is different today in your life? Start by a small thing then expand. I love this. How refreshing! A great way to bring more awareness into our life.

Relax

Take care of yourself, you work so hard all year around, be gentle with yourself, you are precious. Take a moment to put your feet up and breathe. Things will work out just fine. Just relax and trust.

MT vs Tsuboki

Many asked me to clarify the differences and similarities between Metamorphic Technique and Tsuboki so here we go: they are both based on the Principle of Correspondence of Acupuncture which is nothing less than 5,000 years old. Talk about a reference! They are also based on a gentle yet powerful touch simply using my fingers which some have compared to "butterfly wings"...I've been called worse! There are differences as well: MT is applied on feet, hands and head while Tsuboki is applied on face, neck, shoulder and a light grounding on the feet. Also, while MT is going back to the time spent in the womb and the life force is shifting the unnecessary baggage; Tsuboki is working on 8 out of 14 meridians and sticks more to the physical level however as toxins are flushed out, emotional residues can be released as cells do have memories. The big difference in my eyes though is that MT is permanent, the caterpillar does transform into a butterfly and no way back while Tsuboki is not permanent. We all wish the "natural facelift" lasts forever, don't we? Nice try. However regular Tsuboki makes a massive difference to the glow and texture of the skin plus feels like a full body massage for those who are body shy. So, a bit for everyone's taste in a gentle way. Gentleness goes a long way, trust me!

Never broken
Every time you love somebody, they take a piece of your heart. It doesn't make your heart broken, it makes it expand and stretch so next time you love, you have more to give and to receive.

Annual review
When at the end of the year, have a good look back at what you've achieved; the decisions and changes you've made; the progress in so many areas of your life by may be knowing what doesn't work anymore; the level of awareness you've acquired; the power you've gained back by saying no. And much more, I'm sure. Let's be grateful for the people around us who love us; our health and strength; the love we have to give and help we can provide to others...isn't it magical? So now, being the naughty me...what about writing down your goals for next year? By writing them down, you increase by 40% the chance to see them become a reality. Oh yeah!

Re-open

Life experiences can sometimes toughen us up to the point of disconnecting from our heart, switching it off in order not to feel pain or not to feel at all. Here are some gentle ways to open up again what is at the root of everything, either physically or emotionally. Spend time alone at first in order to recognize who you are as you spend so much time running around and living through others. How that makes you feel? It is sometimes difficult to face ourselves. See what comes up and embrace it. As you go within, concentrate on your breathing. Allow this natural movement to clear stuck emotions, simply allow. Emphasize on the exhale as the inhale will always come as a reflex and let go. Whatever comes up, embrace it particularly if you judge it as negative in order to release it. If you fight it, it will build up within which is not the answer. Let go of the unnecessary in order to make space for something new. Ask yourself what you would like? then listen to the answer. Try something new, stretch yourself, challenge yourself, feel alive and know "in your heart" that you are always safe so stay open!

Age

I'm so grateful for the life I've had so far, the various experiences and people I've met, the wisdom and knowledge I've hopefully acquired and the fact that I'm still standing. So what I know is that tough times don't last. They were there to challenge me, stretch my potential and resilience and make me even more appreciative of the good ones. Great times and tough ones revealed myself to myself and that's alright, that's life. So it is not about how much I've changed but how much I've grown. I see too many people worrying about their age. Just embrace who you are. You are beautiful in & out. The heart is never too young or too old. When it comes to love, age doesn't matter. Just be happy!

Now or later

What is the difference between patience and procrastination? If patient, we know like we know we are on the right track and we've done everything we possibly can in order to reach our goal. Failure is not an option. It's just a question of timing but it feels right in our heart. When procrastinating, we just find excuses after excuses with never ending deadlines. And it might feel good for a short while but deep inside, guilt and fear are stepping in. Some might say this is too black & white but guess what, staying on that grey area might just be the exact procrastination spot so get out of here...! Make a decision now, check in within your body and see how it feels. The body never lies but the mind does, it can justify anything!

Daily boost

How to keep your life force, energy, vibration going? Simple daily tips: move your body, connect with nature, drink water, eat vibrant food, get excited about life, meditate, find some space for you physically or mentally, have a goal, tick one thing on your to do list, forgive and let go, be kind to yourself, be aware of toxic people and protect yourself, dream bigger, know you are in the right place at the right time so you find peace for now, receive healing to re-balance or shift when necessary, look within and fall in love with yourself!

Simple

Simplicity is the way forward. Simplicity reduces stress. It goes with awareness of who we are and knowing what we want. It is all about honesty, how we feel towards ourselves and others. Being awake. Trusting this little voice within ourselves. It is about showing our true colors and expressing ourselves. Simplicity allows dialog and helps avoiding judgment, expectation and hurts. Simplicity is the way it should be before we decide to let our ego get involved and try to be clever. Simplicity is smart. So let's keep it simple.

No regret

No matter what happened in your life, have no regret. Coming to London is so far the best decision I've made in my life. It wasn't part of the plan as there was no plan to start with anyway. This way of doing things might not work for everyone however I've learned one thing: with a plan comes expectations and more often than not, disappointment can occur. Getting into action mode then trusting and going with the flow have been so far much more beneficial. It is to be expected within the flow to experience the so-called "as above so below" however those ups and downs do bring you to the perfect destination whatever your dream can be. So let's embrace it all. There's so much we don't know in this world. As my grandmother always said: "Follow your destiny" which is all about going with the flow. There's a bigger plan out there which doesn't mean doing nothing neither however let's release the pressure to figure it all out. There's no mistake as we know, only experience. No time for regret. Let's focus on what has been achieved so far instead, what could be improved and let's have some fun!

Download

Many of my clients come to me exhausted, drained, stuck and the rest of it. Some might say this is the society we live in, the job they have, the family's duties...the list is long. Of course, a session of Metamorphic Technique will give you a chance of a break, recharge your batteries, be clear-minded on what your priorities are and that amazing capacity to smile to the world. However, there are some little tips and tricks to help you along the way. I've noticed it is easy to find ourselves overloaded with information: watching the news in the morning then read them again in the tube and finally read them again in the evening on the way back home...What is that all about? Too much is too much. First how many times do we need to know what is going on in the world in a day? Does our life depend on it? When do we have the time and "mind space" to simply be? How can you create if you are always busy or uploading information. Time to switch off from the bad news and misery and bring in some positivity. I've noticed a clear increase in my productivity as I watch the news in the morning then write on the tube and allow my brain to clear the unnecessary, prepare my day in a positive light bringing my brain to full capacity when I get to work. So less uploading, more space, more creativity, more fun!

Thank you to you all for making my life so extraordinary!
Keep blossoming, you are beautiful!

Printed in Great Britain
by Amazon

34217348R00037